PORT ERIN

Past & Present

CW00924425

RAY STANFIELD

with additional material by

GEORGE HOBBS and SARA GOODWINS

Loaghtan Books
Caardee
Dreemskerry Hill
Maughold
Isle of Man
IM7 1BE

Published by Loaghtan Books

First published: October 2019

Textual copyright © Sara Goodwins, 2019

Typesetting and origination by:
Loaghtan Books

Printed and bound by:
Latimer Trend

Website: www.loaghtanbooks.com

ISBN: 978-1-908060-29-7

Photographic copyright (modern
photographs) © George Hobbs, unless
specified otherwise

All rights reserved. No part of this publication may be reproduced, stored on a retrieval system or transmitted
in any form or by any means without prior permission of the publishers.

Front cover: Port Erin Railway Station, past and present (see also page 51)

Rear cover: One of the caves under Bradda Head

Title page: Snow on the way to Cregneash, looking back at Port Erin

CONTENTS

INTRODUCTION

Postcards were the text messages of the day. Before phones became ubiquitous, the only way to contact friends and relatives who lived at a distance was to write to them. With several postal deliveries per day, it was perfectly possible for a postcard sent to an island address and posted in the morning, to be delivered in the afternoon or evening. Posted early enough and it was even possible to get a reply, all within the same day. And postcards were cheaper to send than letters. Before 3 June 1918, the postage rate for postcards was ½d: for a letter it was 1d. The cost of postage rose gradually, as it still does, but the differentiation of postage between postcards and letters remained until the mid 1960s.

Consequently all sorts of people sent postcards for all sorts of reasons. The old postcard on page 14, for example, was sent to Mrs J. G. Crebbin, Strathallan Hall Cottage Summer Hill, Douglas with 'just a line to let you know Uncle Harry died yesterday afternoon and is to be buried on Wednesday at 2 pm…' Or the writer of the postcard on page 62 had left his map behind, wanted it posted on and explained it was 'in the cupboard either behind the writing materials or magazines.'

Many postcards were sent by holidaymakers, of course, but quite a lot were sent from UK addresses, or at least franked in the UK. Few people at the time had cameras so postcards were souvenirs and reminders of a good time.

Postcards were big business and there was a number of different manufacturers, although Valentine's of Dundee is generally thought to have produced more cards than anyone else. Whoever published the cards tended to use local photographers, however, so cards with Manx views often featured the work of Manx photographers such as T. Keig, C.J. Midwood or, for Port Erin, P.J. Prideaux. There were local postcard publishers too, particularly V.L. Swales of Port St Mary.

CHAPTER 1

ON THE OCEAN WAVE

Boats are important to Port Erin. Before the tourists discovered it, Port Erin was a small fishing village. Only a few hundred people lived here and almost all of them had some connexion with the sea. The village grew at the eastern end of the large bay precisely because it provided boats with excellent shelter from all storms except those from the west.

East of the breakwater (see page 23) the sea bed slopes gently from the harbour until it's covered by about twenty-five feet of water at high tide; beyond the breakwater the bay drops by about another twelve feet. Currents within the bay are negligible but along the coast and particularly in Calf Sound tidal streams are strong. Because the seabed within the bay is a shallow slope of sand and gravel Port Erin was suitable for mooring salvaged wrecks until their future – repair or scrap – had been decided.

The influx of holidaymakers made little difference to the fishing fleet at first, although entrepreneurs started charging visitors for a boat ride, or hiring out rowing boats. Many visitors had a go at fishing from a rowing boat on a calm day, and it wasn't unusual for holidaymakers to present their seaside landlady with a freshly caught mackerel and ask her to cook it for their tea (or breakfast).

The herring stocks in the Irish Sea collapsed in the 1980s, so today Manx commercial fishing is centred on king and queen scallops, and whelks. There are around 70 commercial fishing vessels currently registered on the island, with a further 200 or so from the UK with permission to fish in Manx waters.

All this boating activity meant that a lifeboat was needed. When the Port Erin station opened in 1883, the first lifeboat was the ten-oared *Ann and Mary*, supplied by Richard Roberts of Manchester. She arrived by ship in Douglas and was taken to her new home by her special launching carriage.

The early lifeboats relied on oars – in rough seas sails can be a dangerous handicap – and rowing a heavy boat into wind is both time consuming and tiring, so the usual procedure was to use eight horses to haul the lifeboat on its carriage overland to a convenient beach for launching upwind of where the problem was. The crew could then row with the wind, allowing them to arrive quickly and without being too tired to where they were needed. Fast transportation of the boat by land was practiced nearly as frequently as lifesaving techniques at sea.

Port Erin has had eight lifeboats in total, all crewed by volunteers: *Ann and Mary of Manchester*, *William Sugden*, *Henry Kirk*, *Ethel Day Cardwell*, *Matthew Simpson*, *Osman Gabriel*, *Herbert and Edith*, and, currently, *Muriel and Leslie*. It is RNLI policy to name its boats after the benefactors who have largely paid for them.

Even when volunteers give up crewing the boats, they are often still involved with RNLI operations. Philip Crellin was a volunteer crewmember on the *Osman Gabriel* (see page 11) between 1987 and 1992, and helmsman on the *Herbert and Edith* (see page 7) until 2004. He then went shoreside to become the volunteer Deputy Launching Authority, and is, since December 2017, the Lifeboat Operations Manager. Volunteering is in the Crellin blood; Philip's father Henry also held the position of Lifeboat Operations Manager.

Berthed next to Raglan Pier is *May II*, BA193. She was a Scottish fishing vessel, probably built in the late 1930s by Weatherheads of Cockenzie, East Lothian, Scotland. She's what was known as a ringer, from the ring nets used to encircle a shoal of fish. She was based in Girvan, owned by J&S McCreath and named after Jimmy McCreath's daughter.

The letters in front of the number on the boat indicate its home port. BA tells us that the *May II* in the old postcard came from Ballantrae, South Ayrshire, Scotland. The light blue boat in the centre of the modern picture is a Manx craft: RY stands for Ramsey.

Isle of Man. Port Erin.

The steam-driven fishing boat tied to the harbour wall above is the *Lady Loch*. Steam fishing boats were first developed in the 1870s, although steam drifters were not introduced in the herring industry until 1897. They were more powerful and therefore also larger than their smaller sail driven sisters. Note the large number of boatmen in the picture.

Port Erin is noted for its glorious expanse of beach. Sandy beaches occur in flat areas of coast which collect sediment washed off the land and tossed up by the sea. High tides and wind push the sediment further up the land to the edge of the waves and a beach is born. Shallow bays or estuaries have the largest beaches as the waves are not powerful enough to move the sand away. Beaches can be made up of fine particles of rock, crushed coral or ground up shells, but most are formed of tiny particles of quartz and feldspar.

Today we would talk about pictures being 'photoshopped', but the practice isn't new. In this view the waves don't look at all natural. Not only that but it's doubtful whether the lifeboat would actually be launched with the masts raised and with pleasure boats directly in front of it. What's more likely is that the lifeboat is actually being winched back up the slope into the lifeboat house. The photographer then added the apparent splash of the waves to reverse the action and make it appear that the boat was being launched, thus providing a much more thrilling shot.

The Port Erin lifeboat slipway has one of the steepest slopes of any in Britain. When the Watson-class lifeboat *Matthew Simpson* (see page 9) slid down it, the boat was anticipated to hit the water at about 20mph. The *Osman Gabriel* was Port Erin's last offshore lifeboat, and was replaced in 1993 by inshore lifeboat *Herbert and Edith*, herself replaced in November 2006 by this craft, the *Muriel and Leslie*. The RNLI uses rigid inflatable boats (RIBs) for its inshore fleet, which would be damaged by sliding down a slipway. Consequently the *Muriel and Leslie* rides down the slipway on a launch cradle.

The *William Sugden* was a 12-oared boat under Coxwain W. Callister and the second Port Erin lifeboat, coming into service in 1892. She was 37ft long by 8ft wide, self righting, and cost £544. This doesn't sound much until you realise that a working man at this time was usually paid less than a pound a week. The carriage, which cost £129, was important, not just for getting the boat into the sea but for getting it to the best place to launch (see page 4).

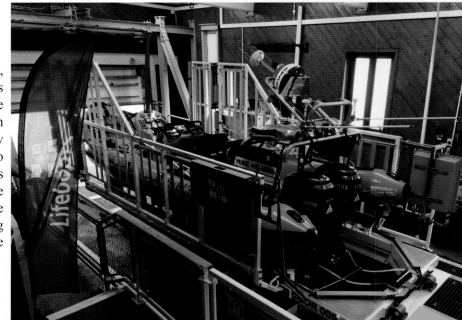

The current Port Erin lifeboat, the *Muriel and Leslie* B-813, is named after Mr and Mrs Leslie Hartle who spent many happy holidays in Port Erin and whose legacy helped pay for the new lifeboat. She came into service on 1 November 2006, but was not officially named until 5 May the following year. Here she is being made ready for practice: her crew are suiting up off camera and the lifeboat house door is being opened in front of her.

The *Matthew Simpson* was the second motor lifeboat to serve at Port Erin, replacing the *Ethel Day Cardwell* in 1939. A 41-ft Watson-class lifeboat, *Matthew Simpson* was on station for thirty-three years, although she did get a new engine in 1963. In 1972 she became part of the relief fleet and was sold in 1976. She spent some time working on the Thames at Leigh-on-Sea, and is now in private hands.

Today Port Erin's lifeboat is B-813 *Muriel and Leslie*, a B Class Atlantic 85 inshore boat with a top speed of 35 knots, making it the RNLI's fastest lifeboat to date. The B class of Rigid Inflatable Boats (RIBs) replaced the A class of small rigid lifeboats for inshore work. 'Atlantic' is named after Atlantic College in Wales where the RIBs were first developed, while 85 indicates the length of the boat: she is 8.5 metres long and 2.8 metres wide. The crew, left to right, are Rob Bennett, Liam Lowry, Tony Mitchell, Cal Qualtrough. *(Photograph courtesy of Jim Gibson, Ellan Vannin Images)*

Lifeboat practice. Note that the crew and shore volunteers are manhandling the boat on the beach (see page 4) as the old lifeboathouse, used from 1884 to 1925, had no slipway. Some lifeboats still have to be launched from the beach, using a partly submersible tractor with a hydraulic trailer which can be tipped to the right angle for the lifeboat to achieve the right momentum to gain deeper water efficiently. This postcard is franked 30 September 1918, so the lifeboat is probably the *Henry Kirk*, which replaced the *William Sugden* in 1912. The *Henry Kirk* saw wartime service, going the rescue of the *Downshire* on 13 February 1915 when it was attacked by enemy submarine and sank nine miles north west of the Calf.

Today's lifeboat is still launched from a carriage, now called a cradle, although the procedure is rather more high tech. An electric winch lowers the cradle containing the RIB lifeboat (see page 7) down the slipway into the water, where the two 115 horsepower engines are started, and the boat pulls away. The cradle is then winched out of the water to await the lifeboat's return. As the boat has to be reversed into the cradle, in very heavy seas the returning boat is occasionally moored by the pier or harbour wall.

This is the new lifeboat house, built in 1925 when Port Erin received its first motor-powered lifeboat the *Ethel Day Cardwell*. The lifeboat house was built by Costain & Cooper and cost £250 13s 0d, which was considerably less than the boat it housed. The notice on the end wall says: 'Royal National Lifeboat Institution' 'LIFE BOAT' 'Supported by Voluntary Contributions'. Nearly one hundred years later and over 90% of the RNLI income is still supplied by donations and legacies from the public, the rest coming from merchandising and investment.

The lifeboat house and slipway were altered in 1972 to accommodate the new lifeboat *Osman Gabriel* which arrived the following year. After nineteen years on station and one year as a relief boat, the *Osman Gabriel* was sold to the Estonian Lifeboat Service, *Eesti Vetelpaasteuhingu*. On 18 March 1993 she was officially handed over and renamed *Anita*, after the wife of the then British ambassador Brian Low. *Anita* is stationed at Haapsalu on the western coast of Estonia.

The 'new' lifeboat house shortly after it was built in 1925. Inclined slipways are used where there is a big tidal range, to ensure that the boat arrives speedily into the water. Until 1993, Port Erin had an offshore lifeboat (see page 7). The composite hull of the lifeboat rested on rollers, but, once released and moving, proceeded under its own weight down the slipway. Note that the floor of the lifeboat house is hinged to allow the boat to drop down.

To avoid too much damage from friction during launch and recovery – which is done by winching the lifeboat back up the slope – it became common practice to grease the slipway. The corollary to this was that the launch became even faster! Today the offshore lifeboat is stationed at Port St Mary. Port Erin's inshore lifeboat cannot slide down the slipway but is lowered into the water in a cradle (see pages 7, 8 and 10).

SS *Greatham*, was built in 1890 by William Gray & Co. Ltd., of West Hartlepool, County Durham as the *Bussorah* for Appleby Thos & Co, also of West Harlepool. Only a year later they sold her to Coombes, Marshall & Co, Middlesbrough who renamed her *Greatham*. This postcard shows her grounded on the Calf of Man and was sent from 'The Homestead, Calf of Man' to Miss Ethel Fargher, 'Ballaqueene' Peel, to wish her 'a very merry Christmas and a prosperous new year, when it comes'.

Grounded on the Calf on 14 May 1911, the *Greatham* is presumably with the ships which freed her. Built as a steam-driven cargo ship with a top speed of seven knots, the *Greatham* became a defensively-armed merchant ship during the First World War, captained by Robert Harrison with a crew of twenty six.

S S *Greatham*, beached at Port Erin awaiting repairs after grounding on the Calf. Unfortunately the repaired ship only lasted a few more years. On 22 January 1918 she was en route from Grimsby, Lincolnshire to Blaye, south west France, with a cargo of coal, when she was torpedoed by U Boat 31 Thomas Bieber. She sank with a loss of seven lives, including two members of the Indian Merchant Service, three miles south east of Dartmouth, Devon.

P ort Erin beach and harbour is used for rather different purposes nowadays! Slacklining is growing in popularity as it's easy to set up and not too difficult because the walker is balanced on a two-inch wide length of flat webbing rather than a thin, round, rope. This slackliner has slung his webbing between the railings on the curve in Shore Road opposite what used to be The Toot (see page 18). The webbing can be tensioned according the walker's preference and acts like a long, narrow trampoline.

The SS *Sabina* was a cargo ship built in 1921 by the German company Friedrich Krupp for the firm Felix De Abasolo of Bilbao, northern Spain. The back of the postcard states that she went ashore at Fleshwick, but history books say the *Sabina* hit rocks around the Calf of Man. Here she is beached at Port Erin awaiting repairs.

A rather smaller boat crosses Port Erin Bay on the incoming tide. Sea kayaking is very popular on the Isle of Man as it offers kayakers the opportunity to view marine landscape, flora and fauna only visible from the sea. Quite often the viewing is two-way as marine fauna such as seals, dolphins and basking sharks also view the kayaker!

Another view of the *Sabina* beached at Port Erin. Her builder, Krupp (see previous caption) later became one of the largest and most successful builder of U boats for the German navy in the Second World War. Somewhat ironically, in 1941 *Sabina* struck a German mine and sank 40 miles off Genoa.

Much of life in Port Erin still revolves around the sea. Here Royal Yachting Association (RYA) training centre 7th Wave Ltd., are taking their Topper Taz and Topper Topaz dinghies into the water for a sailing class. In the background, at the top of the slipway outside the lifeboathouse, the cradle for the lifeboat is awaiting the boat's return from practice (see page 10).

CHAPTER 2

DROPPING THE ANCHOR

Harbours, however attractive, are working areas and therefore need appropriate supervision. The harbourmaster has to arrange berths for regulars and guests, ensure that equipment, including navigational aids, is working properly, advise about currents, pilotage or any harbour-related problem, and uphold the law.

Port Erin harbour is sheltered from all winds except those from the west. To remedy that an outer breakwater was planned, to protect ships moored within the bay. It was built in 1864 by William Powell, at a reputed cost of £77,000. The work was assisted by the Port Erin Breakwater Railway, which was the first steam railway on the Isle of Man and the only broad gauge line; its rails were. more than twice the distance apart of those in Port Erin Station. The works locomotive was housed near what is now the harbourmaster's office.

The breakwater was designed by John Coode – Sir John in 1872 – and stretched for 300 yards (270 m) into the bay, terminating in a concrete platform supporting a lighthouse. For the convenience of loading and unloading ships, a concrete low-water landing pier was also constructed on the breakwater a short distance from the quay and parallel to it.

Coode was probably the most respected harbour engineer of the nineteenth century. He advised on harbours in South Africa, New Zealand, Australia and India, but didn't do too good a job for Port Erin. Using a new building technique, huge concrete blocks weighing from fourteen to seventeen tons each were lowered into place, but were not affixed either to each other or to the seabed. Coode and his team were sure that the blocks were so big and heavy that their own weight and mass would prevent movement. They were wrong.

A major storm on 23 December 1884, only twenty years after the breakwater was built, caused the huge blocks to move, and their grinding together could be heard in the town even over the raging of the wind (see also page 23). The photograph at the top right of page 23 might even have been taken after the storm which destroyed the breakwater; locals and visitors could be inspecting what's left. Coode died in 1892, but there seems to be no record of what he thought about the failure of his groundbreaking idea. Today the remains of the breakwater provide an interesting environment for marine wildlife and divers alike.

If the breakwater was something of a disaster, its near neighbour, the Marine Biological Station was a roaring success. Opened in 1892, and at first housed on the other side of the bay from its more famous site (see page 22) its original remit was to study the migration of herring in the Irish Sea, as fishermen had noticed changes in stock levels. It rapidly became a world-class research establishment and one of the most important marine laboratories in Europe. Within ten years it outgrew its first modest buildings and moved to its new home near the old breakwater in 1902. The first fish hatchery in the British Isles, the Marine Biological Station cultivated lobsters, oysters and plaice from eggs. In a single year 50,000 lobsters and five million plaice were released into the sea.

BRADDA HEAD, PORT ERIN, I. O. M.

The postcard is dated 18 September 1911, when the building on the far left still consisted of shops. It was converted by Professor Herdman, director of the Marine Biological Station (see pages 25-6), opened on 4 January 1917 and named The George Herdman Institute in memory of his son who was killed on the Somme. Colloquially known as The Toot (from insti-toot) the ground floor was a recreation room for fishermen and boatmen, while the upper floor housed the town library. Rules were strict: the library was for men only, and only quiet occupations such as chess, dominoes or billiards were allowed. Alcohol and gambling was also forbidden.

The small building standing alone with double doors open is the original lifeboat house, built in 1884. Note that the pier is missing! The card is franked May 1911, which pre-dates the building of the Raglan Pier by five years (see page 21). Just visible to the left and behind the old lifeboat house is the end of a long low building which is said to have housed the narrow-gauge steam tram used when building the breakwater (see page 23). Among the boats in the bay is one which looks like a floating house. In fact this is a floating platform for bathers, with a hut to provide shade if the sun were too strong. Bathers paid a small fee for using it.

I. o. M. Port Erin, Bradda Head

During the Second World War The Toot was used by the Red Cross to train so-called VADs. The Voluntary Aid Detachment (VAD) was an organisation providing voluntary civilian nurses to military hospitals. The Toot has since passed from public ownership and is now a private house. At the time of writing the old coal shed (ex-tram house) is being used by Foraging Vintners, a craft winery.

IN PORT ERIN BAY, PORT ERIN. I.O.M.

The white-sailed boat in the centre appears to be a catboat; they have a wide beam and carry a single mast well forward. Catboats usually only have one sail, but this one also has a jib sail (the triangular one) attached to a bowsprit (the spar pointing out from the front of the boat) making what is known as a Bermuda rig, sometimes called a Marconi rig. The postcard is franked 25 September 1925, and sent c/o 1 Dale Street, Ramsey: 'Dear Lily, Just a line in a hurry. Winnie is coming to Ramsey on Thursday. She has to be in the hospital by 12 o'clock or as soon as the train gets in…'

Most of the boats shown are varieties of small fishing boats. Almost all have some form of engine and most have dispensed with sails. The harbour and Raglan Pier can accommodate boats with up to 3m draft. Previously commercial fishing around the Isle of Man centred on herring, but herring stocks collapsed in the 1970s and '80s. Today the most valuable catch for Manx registered vessels is scallops.

Raglan Pier during the 1960s. The herring fleet still exists and there is a number of small dinghies available for hire to visitors. Work started on Raglan Pier in 1913, and was completed in 1916. The pier was named after George FitzRoy Henry Somerset, 3rd Baron Raglan who was the Isle of Man's Lieutenant Governor from 1902 to 1919.

Taken on 9 June 2019, scallop fishing boats have replaced herring fishing boats by the Raglan Pier. The Research Vessel *Sula* (see also page 29) in the foreground was used by the Port Erin Marine Laboratory, to check the water quality at the Cypris Station, a long-term monitoring point, 5 km west of Port Erin Bay. In August 2006 R.V. *Sula's* monitoring duties were taken over by Fisheries Protection Vessel *Barrule*.

On the beach on the opposite side of the bay on the left, are what looks like a couple of little houses. These had been first the Port Erin Marine Biological Station and then the mortuary chapel; even today the area is known as Mortuary Beach. In 1902 the Biological Station moved to a new purpose-built building (see page 25) and the smaller of the beach buildings became the mortuary chapel while the larger one was adopted as St Columba's Catholic Chapel. Built on the sands the Catholic Chapel was only used in summer as the sea tended to invade it. In winter Catholics had to travel to Castletown to attend mass. The postcard is dated 19 September 1907. Note there is as yet no pier.

Although it looks like the same jetty, this is a newer and larger replacement stretching further into the bay. The jetty is popular with those wanting to fish, although it's covered with water at high tide. The best fishing tends to be on an incoming tide a couple of hours before and after high water. Typical fish caught within the bay include pollack, wrasse, grey mullet, mackerel and plaice.

Port Erin Bay provides good shelter but is exposed to the west and south west. To offer some protection from storms from this quarter a breakwater was planned. It was designed by Sir John Coode, built by William Powell and, at least in part, financed by William Milner (whose memorial tower is so prominent in these photographs). Construction was aided by the Port Erin Breakwater Railway (see also page 17).

On 23 December 1884, a major storm hit much of Britain, including the Isle of Man. A massive gale including the rare phenomenon thundersnow – where snow falls during a thunderstorm instead of rain – hit Port Erin. The outer breakwater couldn't take the pounding and, by Christmas Eve, the low-water landing stage, concrete platform and lighthouse at the breakwater's end had all fallen into the sea.

BRADDA HEAD PORT ERIN   SWALES

The remains of the breakwater are still crumbling and dangerous to walk on, but are now very popular with divers, partly because they are suitable for novices and partly because of the large variety of marine life which has colonised the scattered blocks. They include sea urchin, wrasse and conger eels.

Showing the breakwater, Marine Biological Station, jetty and pier from across the bay on Bradda Head. Both photographs are taken almost on top of the Bradda Mines, whose engine house is still visible from the breakwater, set into the cliff just above the beach. Walkers on Bradda Head often don't realise that the ground below them is honeycombed with shafts and adits some of which reach 50ft below sea level. The area has been mined for copper and lead since 1200 BC, but larger scale mining began in the early eighteenth century. Commercial mining eventually ceased in 1904.

The breakwater was built to protect ships in harbour, but its ruinous state now makes it a hazard to ships trying to reach harbour safely. The fact that the remains of the breakwater are hidden at high tide was a major factor in the decision to build a guidance light on the beach. The end of the breakwater is marked with a green conical buoy. Entrance to the bay is further complicated by the undersea telephone cable laid between the Isle of Man and Ireland in 1929, which skirts the end of the Raglan Pier and the ruined breakwater.

The Marine Biological Station had its beginnings in 1885 when a group of scientists at Liverpool University wanted a permanent laboratory next to the Irish Sea in order to investigate its marine biology. In 1892 Mr Thomas Clague (see page 89) built a small building for them on the beach below Belle Vue Hotel which he owned. Studying the sea was one thing, but being regularly invaded by it was another, and in any case the premises soon became too small. The buildings later became chapels (see page 22).

In the hope of enhancing the stocks of fish and lobsters for local fishermen, the Manx government partly financed a new purpose-built building, into which the scientists moved in 1902. The laboratory became part of Liverpool University in 1919, although the fish hatchery remained under the control of the Manx government. Professor William Herdman, the leader of the group of pioneering scientists, became the Marine Biological Station's first director.

When the station moved to its new home in 1902, it included a small museum and public aquarium and the Manx government insisted that public access be continued after Liverpool University formally took over in 1919. During the Second World War, Port Erin with Port St Mary became Rushen Camp, a giant internment camp for female aliens and their children. Women science students could receive permits to work in the Biological Station; Bridget Jacobs, for example, a zoology student before she was interned, was in charge of six women collecting seaweed for making agar jelly used in research work.

PLAICE ONE YEAR OLD

The station continued to expand and, by the mid 1980s, was four times bigger than the original building. It became one of the most important marine laboratories in Europe, advising, among other things, on the permissible size of fishing catches. In its heyday the station had a permanent staff of 27 scientists, about 30 resident researchers, and taught about 170 students per year.

In 2006, the changing emphasis of marine research caused Liverpool University to vacate the site it had occupied for more than a century. Since then it has become an eyesore of vandalism and fly tipping, made worse by suspected arson in December 2016. In 2018 Delgatie Ltd., based in Castletown, purchased the site from the Manx Government's Dept. of Infrastructure for £500,000. At the time of writing Delgatie, whose owner, Tom Granger, lives in Port Erin, proposes to redevelop the site with a mix of residential, retail, tourist accommodation and exhibition facilities.

Around 1910, just along from the Bay Hotel on the left, was an unusual 'guess your weight machine'. Ladies would be invited to sit in a swinging chair which made up one half of the giant 'balance'. If the gentlemen in charge couldn't guess the lady's weight within 2lbs she didn't have to pay for the experience. Fun, but not perhaps tactful. This image appears to have been taken when there were few visitors, so perhaps the contraption had not yet been installed for the season.

The Bay Hotel, despite its on-shore location, was closed for ten years, before reopening on 17 December 2001 after considerable refurbishment. The photograph was taken in April 2019 when The Bay was being repainted from pink to blue: the chimneys and the end wall are still the old colour. The bungalow to the left of the hotel is reputed to be built on the site of a summerhouse owned by the Dukes of Athol, Lords of Mann in the eighteenth century.

BAY HOTEL

Despite the heading on the postcard, the view is taken from the pier and not the breakwater. The pair of houses, Beachmount and Highcliffe standing alone on the skyline, were built around 1900. They mark the edge of the area called The Darrag. *Darrag(h)* in Manx means 'the place of oak trees' although there are few if any there now.

Beachmount and Highcliffe have been converted into six apartments but still stand sentinel against the sky. Despite the building's apparent isolation a footpath passes it linking Shore Road with Ballafurt Road.

Raglan Pier was declared open on 12 April 1916 by the island's Lieutenant Governor, after whom it was named (see also page 21). The small lighthouse at the end was built at the same time as the new pier and is still operational, flashing a green light every seven seconds. The concrete skeleton tower is 23 ft high, and topped by a weather vane displaying, appropriately enough, a fishing boat.

Many boats over-winter on land to avoid possible storm damage and allow for necessary repairs. The area near Raglan Pier is one such boat park. In the spring and autumn a mobile crane lifts boats into and out of the water. This photograph was taken on 13 April 2019 so the date for lifting in couldn't be far away. The dark blue boat behind the white one in the foreground, is R.V. *Sula* (see also page 21).

The bathing machines on the Port Erin beach are horse drawn, as most were. It was considered indecent for women to be seen in a bathing costume, so the swimmer would enter the bathing machine fully clothed, change inside, and then the bathing machine would be pushed deep into the water so that the swimmer could get into the sea down steps facing away from the beach. The process would be reversed when the swimmer wanted to leave the sea. A signal that he should tow the bathing machine out of the water would be given to the attendant by the occupant raising a small flag from inside the machine. Note that the white patches on the bottom right-hand corner of the picture are washing spread on the grass to dry.

Many huts are advertising boats for hire, and have oars leaning on them. At one time over 200 boats and 50 licensed boatmen were available to take tourists on the water in Port Erin harbour, more than existed in Douglas. Three women seated in the centre, wearing aprons, are obviously taking a break from work. The one in the middle appears to be knitting while her friends on either side are reading books. Education on the Isle of Man was generally better than in the UK.

15713

PORT ERIN, I. O. M

The area of Port Erin nearest the pier was extensively rebuilt with houses during the early part of the twentieth century. The foreground of the modern photograph gives an excellent view of the roof of the raised bungalow half-way down Dandy Hill!

The post-card, left, is franked 25 July 1911 but seaside pursuits haven't changed that much. Adults are relaxing, chatting and looking at the scenery, while their children paddle, play cricket, build sandcastles or bury each other the sand. About the only real difference is the style – and amount – of clothing!

The photograph on the right shows that the sea wall and lower promenade have now been built, and donkey rides have been added to other seaside attractions. Charabancs such as the one in the foreground (the word is derived from the French *char à banc* meaning 'carriage with wooden bench', and pronounced, in English at least, 'sharra-bang') often brought parties of visitors to Port Erin for the day. Early 'charas' – the one pictured is a later design – were uncomfortable and occasionally unsafe as they tended to be top heavy, but they did provide a cheap means of travel for those on a limited budget.

Above, a further modification of Port Erin's sea wall is visible, with a stone wall about three feet high serving as flood defences for the lower promenade. The largest known tidal range at Port Erin is 19.6 feet and the buildings on the lower promenade, unsurprisingly, are at risk from high tides and storms.

The era of pushing bathing carriages into the sea to retain the bathers' modesty might be over, but the carriages are still in use as stationary beach huts. The row of white fishermen's cottages in the centre were built using money left by William Milner – he of the tower on the headland – for use by the fishermen of Port Erin. They're called St Catherine's Terrace after the holy well near them (see page 126). They were managed by the church for many years before being taken over by the Port Erin Commissioners. The rent of the cottages, after paying for repairs, was to be used to pay for a curate for Rushen.

Shore Road runs between the front doors of St Catherine's Terrace and their gardens on the opposite side. The beach-side gardens are noted for being both pretty and quirky. In recent years many private gardens throughout Port Erin have been opened to the public for one weekend per year, with money raised going to local charities.

The small lighthouse on the beach was built to a lattice-work design when it was first placed there after the storm of 1884. It was constructed to show boats a clear passageway into Port Erin Bay and was needed after the destruction of the breakwater that same year (see page 23). The lighthouse was 34 ft. tall square with a lattice framework and black metal hexagonal lantern as seen here. It formed part of a pair, the other of which was placed on top of a concrete pole on the promenade; the lights in line marked a safe passage into the bay. The two together are known as the Front Range and Rear Range lights.

The current lighthouse on the beach is octagonal, made of concrete and 36 ft. tall. The rear range light has been changed frequently, but is still situated on the promenade on the top of a 15 ft. pole. Both lights are visible for five miles and boats must keep them aligned (at 099°.06) to be sure of safe passage.

CHAPTER 3

FISHING VILLAGE TO SEASIDE TOWN

Port Erin might have remained a fishing village had it not been for the arrival of the railway. The importance of this event is indicated by the fact that Port Erin's main street is not 'High Street' or 'Main Road', but Station Road. Opening to Port Erin on 1 August 1874, the narrow gauge railway meant that visitors could easily get to what was still a village. Once there they liked what they saw and wanted to stay. Before the advent of the railway, Port Erin had only one hotel, The Falcon's Nest (see page 81). If the little town was to capitalise on its new popularity that had to change.

It's difficult to talk about Port Erin without mentioning Mr James Clague who was something of an entrepreneur and property developer. He owned Rowany Farm and married Susannah Moore of Fleshwick Farm, which meant that he had quite a lot of land. He saw the potential for developing Port Erin as a tourist hotspot and built many of the hotels along the promenade on part of his farm. The speculation made him rich and he was able to build a substantial nine-bedroom dwelling, Rowany House for himself and his growing family. It still exists on Rowany Drive next to the golf course. Despite Clague's myriad ventures it's interesting that he lists himself in Brown's Directory of 1894 as 'farmer, fruiterer and car proprietor'. He was obviously wealthy and up to date; startlingly so, if the car mentioned referred to a motor car. Automobiles were only just being developed in 1894 and there would have been only a handful, if that, on the island.

The building firm McArd was founded by Joseph or 'Jos' McArd in Port Erin in 1850. As well as more modest dwellings, McArds built many of the most important buildings in Port Erin including The Hydro (see pages 92-3), Collinson's café (see pages 114-5), the railway station (see pages 50-1) and the Marine Biological Station (see pages 25-6). McArd also worked with Douglas-based architects Horrocks and Lomas on the terrace on the north side of Athol Park (see pages 60-1). Sadly the old firm went into liquidation in 2016.

During the Second World War large parts of the Isle of Man became internment camps for what were termed 'enemy aliens'. This meant that anyone who was a citizen of one of the countries with whom Britain was at war, regardless of how long they had lived in Britain, could be locked up for the duration of the conflict, in case they were spies. Port Erin was the internment camp for women and children. At first, married couples were separated, with the different partners staying in male or female camps, but, on 8 May 1941, a married camp was also opened in Port Erin.

There was little paid work for the female internees so they often made items for sale. A so-called 'Alien's Shop' was opened in Station Road, where handknitted garments, embroidered or lace tablecloths, and other crafted items made by the internees could be purchased. It was next door to what is now Manton's (17 Station Road) but reports differ about which side.

Harvesting was a chore shared by everyone. The horse-drawn vehicle is probably a mechanical reaper, which cut the corn, depositing it in bundles at one side, such as those to the left of the figures. Sheaves would then be gathered and tied by hand before being stooked or stacked vertically so that they could dry in the air. Note the stooks along the far hedge and that the gentleman in the bowler hat appears to be leaning on a scythe. He would presumably use it to get into the corners of the field which the mechanical reaper couldn't easily reach.

Glendown Farm has been in the Qualtrough family for eight generations. Mainly a dairy farm, it also runs some sheep, and offers excellent self-catering and camping facilities to visitors. Film buffs might recognise the farm as, in 2004, it was the setting for the film *The Dark* starring Sean Bean. In the film the Port Erin area was standing in for Wales…

Old aerial photographs (see right) are something of a rarity, given that heavier than air flying machines date from 1903, i.e. after when some of the photographs in these postcards were taken; early photographs were taken from balloons or kites. This card is franked 18 August 1935, so was probably taken from a plane; aerial photography was used in reconnaissance during the Second World War. Milner's house (see page 45) is visible opposite the Falcon's Nest Hotel, the Pavilion (see pages 122-5) stands next to the field in the centre of the photograph and the Methodist Chapel which became the Erin Arts Centre retains its spire.

The photograph is credited to P.J. Prideaux, who was a member of the Isle of Man Natural History & Antiquarian Society, an organisation founded in 1879 and which still exists. He was obviously local to Port Erin as he was secretary of the Port Erin Golf Club on Bradda Head (see pages 68 and 72) in the late 20s and early 30s.

Modern aerial photography is made much easier by the use of drones, although these are still classed as unmanned aircraft – which of course they are – and the Civil Aviation Authority has strict regulations governing

their use. The most obvious thing the modern photograph reveals is how much Port Erin has grown in eighty years. Despite the plethora of Victorian hotels built to accommodate the influx of visitors, in the old photograph Port Erin is still a very small town. *(Modern photograph © Jon Wornham)*

More than a century ago, wheat was cut by hand and bound into sheaves (see page 37). A group of sheaves, often twelve to represent the twelve apostles, was then leant against each other to keep the heads of grain off the ground, away from damp and vermin. Once it had dried and cured a little it would be brought in for threshing. In the distance, Port Erin is expanding up the hill, although there are few buildings as yet behind the promenade. This postcard is franked 7 June 1914 and enquires whether Mrs Rud and Mrs Jackson of Braeside, 25 Lancaster Road, Douglas received the 'box of chocolates and photo of Little Frank, Flo sent on 23/12/13. Love to all Big Frank'

The photograph on the right is taken from near the lower gateway to Ballaman. Built by racing driver Nigel Mansell, the mansion is now owned by billionaire John Whittaker, Chairman of Peel Group, an organisation which invests in property in north west England, particularly the Manchester area. Just visible, bottom right, is the roof of the first house off Ballafurt Road in the Darrag. It is also visible in the old picture opposite.

The photograph above is taken early in the morning from Mull Road leading to Cregneash, which probably explains why beach and roads are deserted. The corner in the foreground on the left is where one of the gateways to the mansion Ballaman now is. The notch visible in the skyline, marks Fleshwick Bay.

Port Erin from the Darrag. The white house in the centre of the foreground is where the artist William Hoggatt lived. Famous, among other things, for designing the memorial window to T.E. Brown, now in the Manx museum, Hoggatt eloped to the Isle of Man with the sister of a friend. He and Dazine Archer were married in Port St Mary on 20 April 1907, despite opposition from both sets of parents. They bought the Darrag farmhouse in 1920 and lived there for the rest of their lives: he died in 1961, she in 1968. In the foreground, just to the left of the white house and close to the centrefold are two figures, a lady in a white dress and a gentleman standing to her left. There is nothing to say that they are William and Dazine Hoggatt, but the hat the gentleman is wearing is exactly the shape of hat favoured by the artist…

The modern image is not taken from exactly the same spot, as the old photograph was taken from what is now private land. The white house visible at the end of the road beyond the road sign, although recently extended and refurbished, is where William Hoggatt lived.

Almost none of these buildings now remain, although the Falcon's Nest Hotel (see page 81) provides a good reference point. As the laboriously climbing figure shows, Strand Road used to run along the front of the Falcon's Nest Hotel, but was extremely steep. The painted sign on the roof says 'T. Qualtrough, Butcher'. Thomas Qualtrough also had premises at Port St Mary.

Several buildings, including the butcher's shop, were demolished to reroute Strand Road along a less precipitous course. All that now remains of the old part of the road is the steep footpath joining Station Road to the lower part of Strand Road.

St Catherine's Church, on the right, was built in 1880 with the aid of £1,000 donated by William Milner in memory of his wife Jane, with the stipulation that the new church was dedicated to that patron saint. It was built on land known as Magher Loch, which Milner owned and which colloquially could be called part of his garden; his house stood where Milner Towers is now.

St Catherine's Church appears little altered, but almost everything else has changed. As tourist numbers have declined many of the old hotels have been demolished and replaced with apartment blocks. Motor traffic has increased and pedestrians are fewer, although not perhaps today. The photograph was taken in March 2019 when the Promenade was closed for resurfacing.

Station Road looking west towards the sea. A 'colourised' postcard, i.e. a black and white photograph which has been coloured by hand. The Falcon's Nest Hotel (see page 81) is the large building in the distance on the left. During the latter part of the nineteenth century its proprietor was George Trustrum, who built most of the shops opposite it. Trustrum was keen to enhance Port Erin as a tourist venue and was also a practical man. He was Chairman of the Sanitary Authority, Port Erin Commissioners, and Secretary of the Port Erin Water Company. Before the arrival of the railway on 1 August 1874, visitors could only reach the small fishing village – which is what Port Erin was – by horse-drawn vehicles along poor roads, or by boat.

Station Road, Port Erin.

The building on the left of the photograph, in front of the Falcon's Nest Hotel, is the old goods shed, now home to the Port Erin Railway Museum. Quite literally at the end of the line, the museum houses a collection of steam locomotives, plus the Royal Saloon which carried Queen Elizabeth the Queen Mother in 1963 and her daughter the Queen in 1972.

STATION ROAD, PORT ERIN.
right.
P.E.6. I.M.

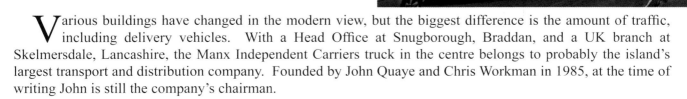

Station Road looking east in another colourised photograph (see top caption opposite). It is obviously a windy day as the canvas awnings are flapping. In the nineteenth century bow-fronted shops were banned as they intruded onto the pavement. To obtain the same amount of display space, shops began to be built with recessed doors and, as glass manufacturing techniques improved, larger windows. Canopy blinds began to be popular to shade goods from fading in the sun, and to provide browsers with shelter from the weather.

Various buildings have changed in the modern view, but the biggest difference is the amount of traffic, including delivery vehicles. With a Head Office at Snugborough, Braddan, and a UK branch at Skelmersdale, Lancashire, the Manx Independent Carriers truck in the centre belongs to probably the island's largest transport and distribution company. Founded by John Quaye and Chris Workman in 1985, at the time of writing John is still the company's chairman.

Port Erin, Station Road.

Station Road looking east. Helpfully, the sender of the card has dated it 15 August 1911, which explains the total lack of motorised vehicles – cars were rare. Fry's chocolate is advertised clearly on the shop window. Fry, Cadbury and Rowntree's were the three biggest British makers of confectionary for most of the nineteenth and twentieth centuries and Fry's chocolate creams were the first mass-produced chocolate bar.

Fewer wheeled vehicles and more pedestrians one hundred years ago made crossing the road, or even standing in it, less dangerous. Today the town is provided with a zebra crossing with accompanying belisha beacons. The beacons were invented in 1934 and named after Leslie Hore-Belisha, the UK's Minister of Transport at the time. The stripes were added to the crossings in 1948 and were apparently named 'zebra crossing' by James Callaghan, Labour MP for Cardiff South, and the UK's Prime Minister 1976-9.

On 11 February 1929 the Isle of Man was hit by a tremendous blizzard with fallen snow quickly cutting off smaller settlements. *Caledonia,* complete with snow plough attachment, is obviously keeping the railway open. Rather ironically the advert far right shows a woman on a sledge enjoying winter sports at Basle. At this time, Patrick Murphey, engine driver, lodged in Ballafurt Road: perhaps he's one of the men in the cab.

Ninety years later, *Fenella* is running round her carriages at Port Erin station in April 2019. The photograph of *Caledonia* above was taken just after the set of points furthest away from *Fenella*; the tree still remains. *Fenella* is one of two locomotives – the other is *Peveril* – to be named after fictional characters. Both names come from Sir Walter Scott's *Peveril of the Peak*, a novel popular at the time and set in Derbyshire and on the Isle of Man.

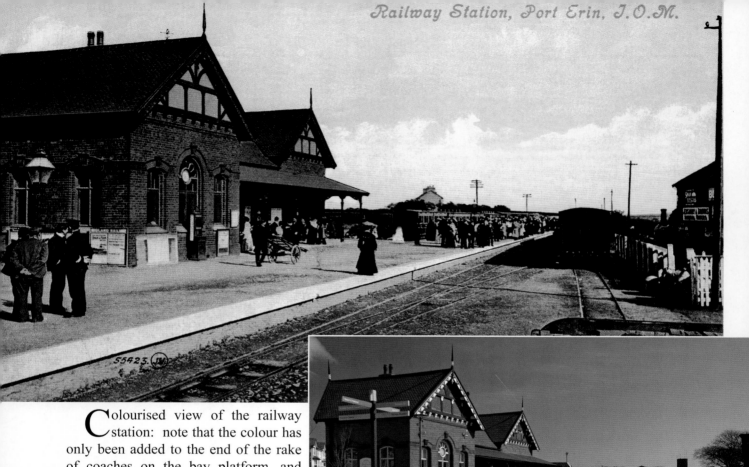

Colourised view of the railway station: note that the colour has only been added to the end of the rake of coaches on the bay platform, and not to their sides. The railway station was rebuilt in 1902, but its completion was delayed by three years as the town commissioners stipulated that the new building should be set further back from the road. The station building is built of Ruabon brick, named after the village near Wrexham in Wales, where the brickworks were situated.

The station was remodelled again during 2016-8, with the most obvious change being the realignment of the track to curve at the headshunt in order to make room for a sloping walkway which leads to the railway museum. The bay platform and siding in the old photograph was removed in 1975 to create the bus depot.

Port Erin railway station was opposite the Station Hotel with the Station Garage next door to that. The hotel had a huge restaurant to cater for the travelling public. T-shaped signs on either side of the wrought iron gates say 'RAILWAY STATION DRIVE SLOWLY'. Early in 1914, Mr Punch of Castletown had thoughts of building a 'Cinematograph Theatre' next to the station where The Haven pub is now. The outbreak of the First World War meant that it never got beyond the planning stage.

The increase in traffic along Station Road led to it being widened in 1974, with the loss of the station's gated entrance. Part of the Station Hotel's huge restaurant is now a fish and chip shop, next door to the prominent sign which reads 'Okell's'. The Port Erin railway station opened in 1874, the same year that Dr William Okell persuaded Tynwald to pass the Manx Brewing Purity Law. Okell, a Cheshire surgeon, founded his brewery in 1850 in Castle Hill, Douglas. The business was purchased by Heron and Brearley in 1972, but the beer still retains the Okell name. Bottled Okell beer is popular in Sweden and Finland.

Locomotive *Fenella* at Port Erin railway station before the platforms were built. The station building shown is slightly smaller than the current one and was built of local stone. It was replaced in 1909 with the larger brick building still in use. Safety at work was an almost unknown concept a century ago; on 1 August 1921, railway employee George Quayle was killed when he fell under a train at Port Erin.

The photographer has not made a mistake: buses are indeed parked on what used to be the railway's bay platform and goods sidings; they were previously housed in what is now the railway museum. Things are always more laid back on the Isle of Man and the railway system is no exception. One famous notice at Port Erin Station said: 'The four o'clock train will be a bus. It will depart at 20 to 5.'

Clague, butchers, c. 1910. Although prominently displayed, the name 'Clague' is actually written onto the image during the printing process. Thomas Clague was a butcher based in Falcon Buildings in 1894, and who also had premises in Bay View Road . The Clague family owned the Rowany Farm and were responsible for developing much of the upper part of the promenade on land they owned (see also pages 92-3). Could Mr Clague be the man obviously in charge on the right?

Davisons is another proudly Manx business, started by Ian Davison in Peel in 1988. Today it involves three generations of the Davison family and has an amazing variety of ice cream flavours. Malteasers, blue bubblegum or blackcurrant and liquorice anyone?

Washing can be seen drying on bushes outside the houses and hotels of Dandy Hill; sometimes it was dried on the beach. Some boarding houses managed to fit a small laundry into the back yard where a coal-fired boiler would heat water for washing sheets and clothes. Small establishments did their washing in the scullery or employed women to take it away and return it clean. Many fishermen's wives would take in washing to supplement their family's income. Regardless of where it was done, it was all done by hand.

The horse-drawn trap is delivering milk in churns. Householders and hotel keepers would bring out their own jugs to buy their requirements. Catering was the most labour intensive part of any boarding house and cooks often got no time off at all during the summer.

Not only most of the buildings, but the gateposts topped with quartz, and even remnants of the iron railings still exist. White quartz is the second-most common mineral in the world (the first is feldspar) and appears frequently on Manx beaches and gardens. Its name comes from the old High German *quarz* which means 'hard'. White quartz seems to have been particularly important on the Isle of Man as, even in antiquity, lumps of white quartz were left in or near graves.

More prosaically quartz is reflective in moonlight so was often used as a primitive form of street lighting. The Isle of Man is proud of its dark skies status and has very little street lighting. Even today, topping a gatepost with quartz can help those out after dark find their way home. Possibly because of its luminous qualities, white quartz was also considered a good luck talisman.

The thatched cottage on the left below, remains on St. Mary's Road as possibly the only thatched building left in Port Erin, although it does now have a dormer window. Thatching on the Isle of Man is usually similar to that in the Highlands of Scotland, Hebrides and North West Ireland. To ensure that the thatch stays put in high winds, it is secured with rope looped around stones protruding from the wall. In the south of the Isle of Man such rope would traditionally be made of straw; in the north it would probably have been made of marram grass known locally as 'bent'.

The green van belongs to SCS or Stewart Clague Services and is quite a long way from home: SCS headquarters is at Baldrine, near Laxey. The firm was founded by Stewart and Barbara Clague in 1969, and is still a family firm with son Alan taking an active role. It is the island's largest building services company.

St. Mary's Road. The Morris Ten is almost certainly stationary and posed for the photograph, but cars were so rare in the 1930s that stopping for a while in the middle of a public road probably wouldn't have inconvenienced anyone. The car registration is MN 8593 and would be considered a cherished plate nowadays with putative owners paying in the region of £2,500 for it. It is not currently issued, which suggests that the car no longer exists. When introduced in 1932, the Morris would have cost less than £200, depending on the variant.

Herring were once plentiful in the Irish Sea and so were a staple of the Manx diet. Manx kippers are usually smoked herring although the term can be applied to any fish which is smoked. The term 'kipper' comes from the Old English *kippian* which means to spawn. Spawning fish are usually abundant, but don't taste very nice, so were smoked to improve the flavour and prolong the time they could be kept. This postcard was produced to advertise John Alldritt's kipper house. The back of the card says that they are 'in season from May to December' and gives a list of prices, the cheapest of which is '7 pairs of kippers (carr. paid) 1/6'. One shilling and six pence is 7½p.

The photographer was unable to locate the exact position of the old photograph, but this view of the Breagle Glen tennis courts looks very similar. As well as tennis, the site includes crown green bowling and crazy golf, although the latter is now very overgrown. The appropriately named Tennis Court House, nearest the camera, is Breagle Glen Bed and Breakfast, noted for the excellence of its cuisine.

Athol Park was named after the Scottish family who inherited the Lordship of Mann in the eighteenth century, and is the only public park in Port Erin. Most of the buildings in this view were developed to cater for tourists. Note Erin House is on the right (see page 104).

Since the old photograph was taken a building, Park Court, has largely filled the space beyond Erin House. Athol Avenue was a footpath to Breagle Glen but is now a private road. At least one of the houses built to provide accommodation for tourists still does so. Athol Park Guest House, formerly The Anchorage, is next to Park Court. Never let it be said that the Isle of Man is not cosmopolitan. At the time of writing, two of the language spoken at Athol Park Guest House are Mandarin and Cantonese.

thol Park is a small glen with a stream running down the middle. The glen remained largely natural until the Second World War, when more formal paths and gardens were laid out by internees imprisoned on the Isle of Man.

he foliage has grown up considerably making Athol Park a pleasant place to sit. Slate slabs bridge a stream which goes under Glen View Road, through a culvert by the back gardens of Strand Road and under Shore Road before reaching the sea by The Quarterdeck. A square seating area, the wall around the Quarterdeck was built in 1951 as part of the Festival of Britain. Episodes from Port Erin's history are carved into the stone timeline.

Port Erin, Athol Park.

The line of houses on the north side of Athol Park is not yet complete. The buildings in the background viewed through the gap, are on Station Road. The larger one on the left with the central dormer window no longer exists. It was replaced in the 1970s by a lower building, which currently houses a branch of the Isle of Man Bank (see page 47).

At the north eastern end of Athol Park (on the photographer's right) is a popular children's playground fenced off from the railway line. There is a public right of way into Athol Park across the long station platform and over the tracks. Long trains have to uncouple and leave a gap between carriages, so as not to block the right of way. Today this rarely happens as trains are generally shorter.

Much of the development along Bay View Road dates from between the wars, but holiday accommodation was advertised in the road as early as 1903. This card was posted on 18 July 1932 from Overdale, which the writer explained 'adjoined the end one on this card. It is just off the picture.' The rest of the space was taken up requesting that the recipient send on the ordnance map they had forgotten to bring with them.

This view is taken from slightly further up the road in order to include the house Overdale mentioned by the writer of the old postcard, which still exists. Between 1899 and 1927 Bay View Road was also the site of the Port Erin Infants School. Until 1905 the school was noted for having no heating.

Judging by the hats this view of the promenade is taken during the 1920s. Most of the hotels on the left were designed by George Kay who arrived in Ramsey from Southport in 1880. He designed the boarding houses on Ramsey's Mooragh Promenade and was soon taking commissions all over the island. The enormous pole in the centre of the photograph appears to be a very large flag pole, although there is a second one outside the town in the distance. They seem a bit public for a radar installation so what on earth are they?!

At the time of writing most of the old hotels on Port Erin Promenade have been demolished and are being replaced by modern flats and apartments. Unfortunately the line and appearance of the new buildings often doesn't blend in with their older neighbours, nor do they tend to use local building materials.

A colourised version of a black and white photograph, where the colourist has used some artistic licence. The front range light on the beach for example, is recorded as concrete lattice work with a black metal lantern. There is no record of it ever being red. Note that horse droppings on the road indicate the usual means of transport!

It is unusual for a road to revert to grass but that's what's happened here. The track gives a better view of the sea and harbour than is obtained from the Promenade, so visitors wanting to enjoy sea views and breezes were often driven along it in horse-drawn carriages. As it was not open to motorised vehicles however, it reverted to being a footpath.

A number of huts around the island – the one on the left here, various ticket offices and huts on the Manx Electric Railway (MER), shelters in Glen Helen, etc. – were made to look 'rustic' by fixing short pieces of split branch onto the outside of wooden walls and then painting them. The original MER huts in Laxey station were installed in 1899, while the appearance of the front range lighthouse (see page 35) shows that this little summerhouse was of a similar era. It's tempting to think that the same Manx firm was supplying rustic huts all over the island.

The cliff slope has been remodelled since the old photograph was taken making it impossible to take a matching shot from the same spot. The grass growing thickly on the sandy cliffs not only looks good but helps stabilise them as the plants' interconnecting root systems act as a mesh to trap particles of sand.

The name 'Spaldrick' possibly comes from the Old Norse *spalar-vik* meaning a narrow gorge. The cottage just visible on the right of the old photograph is Spaldrick View. An old fisherman's cottage, in 1894 it was inhabited by Edward and John Crebbin and is still owned by the same family today. The Headlands and The Towers hotels are in the centre on top of the cliff (see page 96).

The start of the footpath is clearly visible in the old photograph although today it's covered by trees. Footpaths snake their way down to the beach but also lead into Bradda Glen. The archway above the entrance to the glen is made of local Manx slate.

The old postcard is franked 9 September 1909 and, as can be seen from the lamp in the middle distance, Port Erin has street lighting, fuelled by gas. Port St Mary, which was the more important of the two villages at this time, received its gas lighting in 1898, so perhaps Port Erin's was installed at the same time. The two pedestrians appear to be shielding their faces as though hoping not to be recognised. Or is it merely that they are holding their hats against a very windy day?

120 years later, the roads have been very much widened and cars have replaced pedestrians. Beyond the entrance to Bradda Glen, the Bradda East Road now cuts across the field it formerly went round. Part of the old road is now the drive to what was the Bradda Hotel (see page 97).

By the time this photograph was taken The Hut (see pages 116-8) was probably owned by George Trustrum as the rectangular buildings on the headland are probably those purchased by him from the Alien Internment Camp at Knockaloe in 1920. Re-erected by Thomas Costain, Trustrum had a parquet dance floor installed in his new building and ran it as a dancing pavilion in conjunction with The Hut now a café (see pages 116-8). Trustrum's establishment proved a popular rival to Collinson's Café on the other side of Spaldrick Bay.

Bradda Head and Bay, Port Erin, I.O.M.

Probably the most famous view of Port Erin is one which includes Milner's Tower. William Milner was a Liverpool locksmith and safe maker who first visited Port Erin to convalesce, fell in love with the town and eventually spent much of his time there. His house was called, appropriately, The Rest, and was built on the Pulta (see page 81). An apartment block called Milner Towers has replaced it. Milner was a great benefactor to the poor and the tower was built in his honour in 1871. Its shape, when viewed from the top, is said to be that of the key and keyhole used in his safes. It was rumoured that the money collected by public subscription didn't quite foot the bill for the tower and Milner himself made up the shortfall. He died in 1874.

The two ladies in the old photograph have hired their boat from one of the many local boatmen and are exploring Spaldrick Bay. Rowing is good for health and fitness as it is one of the few activities which exercises all major muscle groups. It was also one of the few sports which were considered suitable for women in the late nineteenth and early twentieth centuries. Just visible across the bay is the Traie Meanagh swimming pool.

The wreck of the Traie Meanagh Baths (see pages 110-3) makes this view far less scenic. However there is good fishing off the rocks on the photographer's side of the bay, where anglers might catch coalfish, pollack, wrasse, grey mullet, mackerel and conger eel. Port Erin also hosts an annual sea kayaking event, usually in July, weather permitting.

Spaldrick Bay. The balcony, bottom left, is that of Collinson's Café (see pages 114-5). The roof just visible poking out of the trees on the far side of the bay is The Hut (see pages 116-8). It was built during the mid-nineteenth century as a holiday home for Charles Jennison, part owner (with three brothers and a sister) of the Bellevue zoological and pleasure gardens in Manchester. The Hut was used as a club house, possibly by James B. Thorpe, before being taken over by George Trustrum (see page 46) in 1920 and turned into a café.

Bathing huts and beach tents are a feature of the beach in the photograph opposite, and, just visible, are blobs of white on hedges in the distance, which is laundry drying. Providing and washing bathing towels and renting bathing huts was another entrepreneurial scheme run by James Clague (see page 93). The postcard is written to Master and Miss Lowe and carries 'affectionate greetings from Uncle. It would be jolly if you were here…' It is franked 6 March 1917. Perhaps uncle was convalescing from war injuries?

Possibly the old photograph opposite was taken from out of a window in Collinson's Café; the new one from Bradda East Road. 'Bradda' probably comes from the Old Norse *bratt-höfuð* meaning steep headland; Bradda Head rises to a height of 382 feet. Under government management since 2009 – before that it was managed by Port Erin Commissioners – Bradda Glen is visible across Spaldrick Bay, and is home to one of the Manx coastal viewing sites. The Manx Wildlife trust has provided information boards and static binoculars to help identify what marine wildlife visitors are likely to see. Bradda Glen's site has been designed to be wheelchair friendly.

The huts in the foreground form the pavilion of what was an eighteen hole golf course on Bradda Head (see also page 68). It opened in 1920 as an alternative to the more prestigious, and probably more expensive, Rowany golf course (see pages 108-9). However the Rowany course had better facilities and was closer to Port Erin and the Bradda Head course closed in the 1950s.

After nearly seventy years, most traces of the old golf course have disappeared and the headland is largely covered by grass and gorse. Gorse appears to flower all the year round, but this is because different species flower at different times. Common gorse flowers from January to June, while Western Gorse flowers in late summer and autumn. Perhaps surprisingly, gorse is a member of the pea family.

Traction engine with threshing machine at Bradda Farm run by Mr Crebbin. During the later nineteenth century mechanical threshers gradually became more common, reducing the time and manual labour needed to thresh a crop. The threshing machine, powered by steam traction engine, would travel around to all farms in turn, with farmers and their workers all lending a hand to help neighbours. Note the gentleman (possibly Mr Crebbin?) holding his daughter by the ankle to keep her safe as she perches on the traction engine for the photograph.

The photographer was unable to locate the exact position of the old photograph, but this modern view of farm buildings and Crossfield Cottage looks similar and, judging by the skyline, is not too far off. The buildings and walls visible are almost all made of stone, a material readily available on the island and so used most frequently. It's difficult to shape and split without great effort so many structures, particularly farm buildings, were built of rubble walling which was often very wide to accommodate very different sizes of stone.

CHAPTER 4

PLACES TO STAY

One factor which affected the whole of the Isle of Man was the North of England tradition of Wakes Week. From June to September different manufacturing towns were on holiday each week, although the holidays were unpaid. The mills and factories in a town would close, and their workers would go on holiday, usually together.

The postcard opposite, for example, is franked 4 August 1906. The writer didn't sign their name, but did ask the recipient, Mrs White of Swinton, Near Manchester 'how do you like my hotel?' and comments that they 'saw a few Swinton people today'. The workers of Swinton had obviously deserted their home town and filled up those on the Isle of Man. Between June and August 1913, for example, over 600,500 visitors came to the Isle of Man, twelve times the island's population at the time. Sea bathing was popular as it was thought healthy and the Isle of Man was considered temptingly exotic. Almost 'abroad'! It was also near enough – and affordable enough – to get to easily.

Electricity only arrived in Port Erin in the 1930s so hotels were lit by gas, boarding houses by oil lamp and servants went to bed by candlelight. Before the days of piped water, water jugs for the hotels' bedrooms and tables were filled from local springs. St Catherine's well (see page 126) was particularly popular as it had a reputation for freshness and even healing properties. Port Erin welcomed everyone, but had a reputation for catering for families.

One facet of hotel residence that we would find unusual nowadays is that private hotels and boarding houses would offer what was known as 'board residence', where the landlady would cook the food her guests themselves had purchased. Obviously, if she had more than one family staying, or a group of single guests, this could mean cooking a variety of different meals.

People staying elsewhere on the island would often spend a day at Port Erin and so required lunch when they were there. Two establishments, Allandale and Sunnyside in Station Road, were particularly popular. Both were run by Miss Paul who ensured excellent home-cooked food at an economical price by the simple expedient of cutting down on variety. The menu was always roast lamb, potatoes and peas followed by apple pie and custard, although she did offer afternoon tea as well.

It was also quite usual for the husband to go to work or run a business, while his wife catered for seasonal visitors. For example, Porter's Directory of 1889, lists builder Joseph McArd (see page 83) as living at West Cliff. His wife, at the same address, was advertising 'select private apartments'. Five years later, in Brown's Directory of 1894, McArd has moved to Windsor House (see page 83). Possibly his wife was then managing the new hotel.

Falcon's Nest Hotel, probably at this time owned by George L. Trustrum (see also page 70) who catered for family and 'commercials', i.e. travelling sales reps. Falcon's Nest was originally called the Port Erin Castle Hotel and built on the site of the Queen's Arms. Falcon's Nest opened in 1860, which predates the railway by fourteen years, and is the oldest hotel in Port Erin. Built by R. Cain and designed by Arther Holme it was extended, in 1882, after which it had thirty-two bedrooms and stabling for fifty horses. Opposite the hotel was a field called the Pulta because it was on the edge of the cliff. Pulta or sometimes, Fulta, is derived from the Manx *failtach* meaning cliff.

The Promenade. The Balmoral Hotel is on the far right with accommodation above and small shops below. It is one of the hotels built by James Clague (see page 36), but was managed by Thomas Taylor. Mr Clague also owned the shops, one of which was a greengrocers selling produce grown on his farm. The postcard is franked 17 July 1933 and carries the message: 'John is sunbathing and not looking quite decent.'!

White quartz has many uses on the Isle of Man (see page 55) including occasionally as boundary markers. It's just possible that that was its use here, as the upright standing stone in a line beyond the two piles of quartz marks the original boundary of the lawn belonging to what became the Falcon's Nest Hotel. The Balmoral is now a guest house but still welcomes visitors to its family-run establishment.

Windsor House. Built by Joseph McArd in 1894, as the date at the top of the building proudly confirms. This postcard was posted on 2 January 1933. The message is interesting. Addressed to J.J.M. Card Esq., Croften, Port Erin, it says: 'Several slates, etc., off roof at this address, and [unreadable word] are being damaged. Your attention will oblige. Yours truly John H. Begg.' Presumably 'J.J.M. Card' was really J.J. McArd, i.e. the builder!

The new incarnation of Windsor House was completed in 2014. Designed by Hugh Logan Architects and built by Hartford Homes, the building comprises nine open-plan apartments each surrounding a central kitchen. It's a pity the building doesn't blend in better.

Seaforth House, managed by Mrs Hudson. The hotel was built on part of a parcel of land purchased in 1896 by Joseph Qualtrough (he became MHK for Castletown in 1919 and Speaker of the House of Keys in 1937). He was obviously something of a speculator – what today might be called an entrepreneur – as he divided his land into eleven plots, ten of which he sold to private individuals for them to build hotels and guest houses. The eleventh he sold to the Wesleyan Trustees for £450; the church can be seen behind the hotel. This postcard is franked 2 August 1914, so the building cannot be very old here; it was opened in 1911.

The demolition gives a clear view of the old Methodist chapel. Officially opened on 16 February 1911 by the man who had sold the land, Joseph Qualtrough, it served its Methodists hearers for nearly sixty years. It was eventually sold for £3,000 and became the Erin Arts Centre in 1971. The imposing steeple visible in the old photograph was erected at the expense of Joseph Qualtrough in memory of his father; it was removed in 1983. During the Second World War the Wesleyan schoolroom attached to the church was used as the post office for the Port Erin internment camp.

Seacombe. The proprietor at the beginning of the century was Thomas E. Maddrell who offered 'board, partial board or lodgings; good cooking and attendance'. The figure in the foreground is wearing a fox fur and a cloche hat and reading a newspaper. Behind her head and on the other side of the road, a working class woman and a small boy are just visible propped on the wall outside the railings of the hotel. The woman is holding some sort of box on a stick – it might be a broom – although if she were waiting to be admitted for work, she would surely be at the *back* door. The postcard is franked 31 August 1926.

Fashions in names change for hotels just as much as anything else and Seaforth (see opposite) and Seacombe became Grosvenor and York House respectively. Both were demolished in 2018. Redmayne Investments Ltd were granted planning permission in 2014 to replace the Victorian hotels with a block of fifteen flats but subsequently sold the hotels to Grosvenor Holdings. At the time of writing the new owner's plans for the site have not been published.

BAY VIEW HOTEL ◆ ◆ ISLE OF MAN ◆

Built on land owned by the Clagues of Rowany Farm (see page 36), by 1900 James Mylrea and his wife were offering private apartments in Bay View House. Unlike The Stanley, Myrtle and Erin House (see opposite and pages 103 and 104 respectively), where views of the hotels are included with generic views of Port Erin, this postcard of the Bay View Hotel displays hotel interiors as well as the view visitors can expect of the beach. The building may have been Victorian, but the décor by this time is typical of the 1960s.

The outside of Bay View looks much the same, but the inside has changed beyond all recognition. Now visitors can enjoy spacious open-plan rooms with the most modern appointments. In one respect things haven't changed however. Waterfront, which manages Bay View, like James Mylrea, still takes pride in offering its visitors comfortable and modern sea front apartments.

The STANLEY PRIVATE HOTEL
CENTRAL PROMENADE
PORT ERIN *Isle of Man*

'Phone 3 1 3 4

H. E. Howorth, Ltd., Fleetwood

This view of The Stanley is just the middle panel from a commercial postcard. Entrepreneurial hoteliers would take up offers from equally inventive postcard producers to have their establishment included as a centrepiece in a postcard containing stock local views. This postcard was one of the Arrow Series produced by HEH Ltd. Perhaps surprisingly, the name of the photographer and not the hotel's proprietor appears below the image. H.E. Howorth Ltd., of Fleetwood is the HEH of the Arrow Series.

After so much demolition and change it's nice to see that some of the Victorian hotels remain to grace Port Erin's promenade. Now called Sea Front Holiday Flats, the old hotel has been a family business for forty years. It's recently been renovated to provide seven self-catering apartments.

Snaefell Private Hotel. Built by James Clague (see page 36), in 1904 it had forty bedrooms and was being run by Mrs J. Page. The postcard is franked 3 September 1926 and by this time the proprietor is T.N. Scott, who may be the gentleman just visible sitting with his wife in the doorway of the hotel. Impossible to see reproduced at this size, but, using a magnifying glass on the original postcard, a maid is just visible peeping from behind the curtains in one of the upper windows of the tower. Let's hope she didn't get told off when she should have been working! A window on the top right has a small X next to it, marking the room of the sender. 'W' from Wallasey is having a 'topping time'!

Once again the Victorian Hotel has been demolished and replaced by apartments. Almost all the development of Port Erin Promenade has taken place since about 2005, which is a big change in a relatively short time. Many of the styles of the new apartment blocks attempt to emulate the buildings they replace. At the end of its life the hotel was called the Port Erin Countess Hotel (see page 90), but the new building has reverted to the older name.

Stayed from Saturday Aug. 26th to Sunday Sept. 1st /05.

"Manx Sun" Series. 161

Belle Vue Hotel. The hotel was built by Thomas Costain in 1885 for Mr Clague, the father of Thomas Clague the butcher (see page 53). His granddaughter, Mrs Wyn Rowell, says of the Belle Vue: 'staff and students from Liverpool University stayed. They badly wanted a building as a small Biological Station… so my Grandfather agreed to erect a small building down the cliff from the Belle Vue Hotel and charged the university a very nominal rent…' The front of the post card is inscribed 'stayed from Saturday Aug 26th to Sunday Sept 1st 1905' However that length of time (six days) would be Saturday to Friday, which was indeed 1 Sep 1905. Friday or Sunday, first or third? We'll never know now.

The Belle Vue became the Port Erin Royal and, in 1932, had eighty-five bedrooms and fourteen bathrooms – basins and jugs in the rooms would be the norm. It finally closed its doors in 2008. The building was purchased by property developer Dandara and demolished towards the end of 2017. Dandara commercial director David Thomas comments: 'we have planning permission for new apartments and redevelopment is an opportunity to improve the appearance of the promenade by constructing sympathetic residential accommodation which will also meet demand for new homes.' Redevelopment work started in August 2019, as this book was going to press.

THE TYNWALD.

The Tynwald Hotel was another of the hotels built by James Clague (see page 36) and had thirty-six bedrooms. By 1894 it was owned by Edward Maddrill who sold it in 1911 possibly to Mr and Mrs L Crighton and Mrs Crighton's sister Miss A.E. Latimer. Certainly they owned it in the early part of the twentieth century. The postcard is franked 4 July 1906, so Mr Maddrill would have been the sender's host.

The new proprietors of the Tynwald gradually bought the neighbouring boarding houses until the hotel encompassed the whole block and had sixty-five bedrooms plus a ballroom. The sender of the postcard says: 'Settled in at the Hotel which all looks much the same as last year apart from a newly built swimming pool which has been in use for two weeks!' The card is franked on 2 August 1975, but uses a UK stamp, which is interesting considering that the Manx Post Office – with its own stamps – came into being on 5 July 1973, more than two years earlier.

At some time the hotel's name was changed to the Golf Links Hotel. When Port Erin with Port St Mary became a giant internment camp during the Second World War, this was where pro-Nazi women were housed.

By the 1980s the hotel had been renamed yet again as the Port Erin Princess Hotel. The same company also owned the Port Erin Countess Hotel (see page 88) and renovated both hotels during 1984 and 1985. However, the Golf Links Hotel limited company, set up on 5 May 1978, was not dissolved until 2009, probably when plans were made for the hotel's demolition and redevelopment.

The Imperial Hotel was built in 1938 and said to have over fifty bedrooms. Unfortunately its opening coincided with the beginning of the war so most of its first guests were internees. It was even rumoured that a large number of German prostitutes had been interned here! However not all those staying at the Imperial were ladies of dubious reputation. Elizabeth Bremer was billeted there until 1941; she was a teacher in Liverpool before being interned.

The Imperial re-opened on 25 May 1946 after extensive redecoration which included 'Vita glass in the Sun lounge'. The hotel was demolished in 2007 and, in 2008, work began on a new block of apartments called Imperial Heights. For once what has replaced the old hotel looks better than the original.

Below, the site of the demolished Hydro, looking south east. The building on the far right is the Princess Towers (see page 90). The bottom photograph is the site looking north east. The building on the far left is the Imperial Heights (see page 91).

Above, the Hydro looking south east. The card is franked 16 September 1911, and the two sections of the building nearest the photographer were built some time during 1910-11, so this postcard may have been produced to celebrate their recent completion. The portly gentleman with watch chain and the younger man in a boater standing in the porch, may even have been the proprietor and his son. The Hydro was noted for having a coloured glass ceiling which gave it the feel of a 1930s transatlantic liner.

Hydro looking north east. James Clague, brother of Thomas Clague the butcher (see page 53), owned Rowany Farm and, in 1890, built the first part of the Hydro – it was later extended – on his land. Assisted by J.J. McArd, Clague used stone from Gramma Quarry, which now forms part of Rowany golf course (see pages 108-9). His venture was successful and he went on to build the Snaefell, Tynwald, Balmoral and Imperial Hotels (see pages 88, 90, 82 and 91 respectively). It probably helped that he was, for many years, Chairman of Port Erin Commissioners.

During the Second World War, Port Erin with Port St Mary became a giant internment camp, Rushen Camp, for female aliens and their children. The Hydro Hotel became the camp's HQ, with its ground floor converted into a hospital and maternity unit. Nursing staff were headed by a nursing sister who reported to Dr Margaret Colls a Home Office doctor sent from London to take charge of the internees medical needs.

The word 'Hydro' comes from hydropathy which is a system of treating illness using water, and was extremely popular a century ago. Hydro became a fashionable name for hotels either offering some form of cold water treatment or which were near areas popular for sea bathing. Hydros gradually began to be thought old fashioned, however, and the Port Erin Hydro became the Ocean Castle. It closed in 2007 and was demolished in 2010.

The Peveril Hotel on the Brows above the bathing pool. The card is franked 5 September 1939 and the sender comments that 'this is a good view of our house', so was presumably staying here. By 1962 the hotel was owned by Tom Cubbon Faragher who was MHK for Rushen 1965-76. His son, Charles Harry Faragher, who was also MHK for Rushen 1982-6, continued running the hotel until 1987 when he sold it to open a gift shop.

The company running the Peveril Private Hotel was dissolved on 12 August 2009. Now called The Brambles, the old building has been converted into apartments. Nice to see that it's not been knocked down.

The slightly darker building on the left, is where the sender was staying: 'This is a good view of our hotel… it is two houses thrown into one. We are very comfortable and happy here…' Surprisingly he doesn't mention the name, but it was the Carlton Private Hotel. From 1940 to February 1941 the famous sculptress Erna Nonnenmacher was interned at the Carlton.

The company running the Carlton Private Hotel was dissolved on 8 February 1980 and today, like The Brambles (see opposite), the building is now the Carlton apartment block. It contains thirteen spacious apartments.

The Headlands hotel on the left with The Towers next door. The demarcation is clearly marked by the different shades of the wall next to the road. The Towers Hotel was run by the Keggin family and was where Dr Ingeborg Gurland was billeted when interned. She had been a lecturer at Durham University and became the head teacher of the internment camp school.

At some point the Headlands Hotel must have been purchased by the Keggin family as, in 1996, they demolished both hotels and built the Rowany Cottier Guest House instead. The third generation of the Keggin family still welcomes guests to it.

Bradda Private Hotel. Originally a two-bay building (see page 68) it was extended in the early twentieth century, possibly in the 1920s. Despite appearances, the 'Bradda' prominently displayed facing the photographer on this picture is actually written on the negative before the postcard was printed: the name is above the window to the right. The hotel was particularly popular with golfers as it was situated between the Rowany Golf Course and the one on Bradda Head (see pages 108-9 and 68 respectively).

The hotel closed around 2005 and, at the time of writing, is derelict and decaying. Somewhat controversial approval was granted at the end of 2018 for the old hotel – now called Spaldrick House – to be demolished, and a 72-bed care home to be built on the site. The plans include three villa-type buildings linked together, off-road parking, an alteration of the public highway and a sensory garden.

Bradda Boarding House, Port Erin, I.O.M. *facing sea*

Interestingly, this card, franked on 26 July 1912, was sent to show off the premises and explain the terms and facilities. Annotated on the front with 'facing sea', the back is handwritten by the proprietor and says: 'Dear Sir, Terms are 5/6 in August, with large recreation room in the garden for dances, concerts, whist, etc. Also tents in the garden for gentlemen to camp out. The house is as you turn round to Bradda Head, 5 min. from Spaldrick Bay. I have a large front bedroom terms 6/6 inclusive. Challinor' A Mrs Challinor was listed in Brown's Directory of 1894 as living at Bradda House. I wonder whether Mr Sidney Taylor of Blackley, Manchester preferred the tent or had finances sufficient to stay in the large front room.

The main building of the Bradda Holiday Camp became the Baycliff Hotel, whose proprietors were, for many years, Mr and Mrs Moore who offered special terms to golfers as their hotel was near the course. The hotel boasted a recreation hall which made it suitable for conversion to a youth hostel, so the Bradda Head youth hostel (see opposite) opened here in 1955 replacing the one in Ballasalla. In 1964 adult guests could stay overnight for the princely sum of three shillings and six pence (3/6 or 17½p). The hostel could accommodate eighty guests and had a basic store where touring guests could buy non-perishable food. It was open from 1 March to 30 September, but would open during the winter months for parties of fifteen or more who had pre-booked.

"BAYCLIFF" Y.H. BRADDA HEAD

The Bradda Head Youth Hostel closed at the end of the 1974 season. There was some doubt about its closure so it was included in the 1975 Youth Hostel Association handbook, but didn't open that year. Repairs and renewals had meant that the hostel had run at a loss for the previous three years and the building leaked badly. It also needed rewiring and other work to adhere to fire regulations. After standing empty for a short while it was demolished and a private dwelling built on the site.

The annotation 'facing sea' on the card opposite doesn't really do justice to the spectacular outlook guests would have enjoyed. From here there is a panoramic view over Port Erin Bay, much of the southern coast of the island, and the Calf of Man.

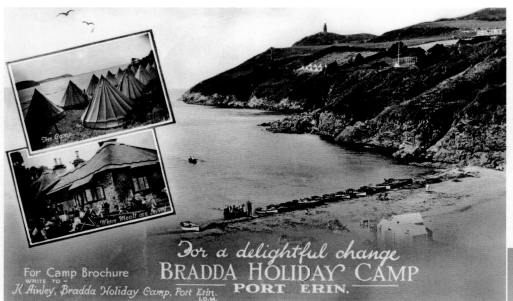

For a delightful change
BRADDA HOLIDAY CAMP
PORT ERIN.

For Camp Brochure
WRITE TO —
K Ainley, Bradda Holiday Camp, Port Erin.
I.O.M.

The Camp

Where Meals are Served

As for the card on page 98, terms are also given on the back of this card, but printed above the space for the written message: 'Bradda Holiday Camp, Port Erin, I.O.M. (run in connection with Collinsons (I.O.M. Ltd.) cafés). A very beautiful and sheltered situation on the slopes of Bradda Head. Weather proof

tents, electrically lighted, carpeted floors, linen and well sprung beds, ample lavatory accommodation & shower bath, private bathing beach. Write for terms to Collinsons Ltd., Port Erin I.O.M.'

In 1929 Collinsons, owners of The Hut (see pages 116-8), decided to centre a holiday camp around it. At first it was for men only; tents provided sleeping accommodation with The Hut as their dining room. However it was so successful that, two years later, the camp was expanded to include ladies, who would eat with the men, but sleep in wooden chalets subdivided into cubicles. As the terms make no mention of sleeping other than in a tent, the old card probably dates from between 1929 and 1931.

During the Second World War the chalets in the Bradda Head holiday camp were used by interned married couples, although at least two nuns, Luise Freitagsmuller and Josefine Franz were also interned there. Both from Germany they had been living at a convent in Hendon when war broke out.

Bradda Road, West, Port Erin, I. o. M.

Mafeking Mrs. T. Clague   Manchester House Mrs. J. Chaloner

On the left, Mafeking run by Mrs T Clague; on the right Manchester House run by Mrs J Chaloner. The card, a 'Manx National Postcard', is published by The Manx Sun with instructions and admonitions in Manx on the reverse: '*Scrieu dty Lettyr ayns shoh* (Write your Letter here)' and '*Yn Ennym as yn Ynnyd-Vaghee dy ve scruit er y cheu shoh* (The Name and the Address to be written on this side.)'.

The short road of six pairs of houses, two of which are Mafeking and Manchester House, which make up Meadowfield appear to have been built as a speculative venture. The houses were ahead of the their time in many ways however. In 1914 they and the rest of that area were supplied with mains water at a cost to Port Erin taxpayers of £200!

May Bank, landlady Miss Corkill on the left; Nottage Cottage, landlady Mrs E.J. Elliott on the right. Presumably the two proprietesses co-operated to fund the production of the postcard. The printed address is given as 'South Promenade'; obviously the two ladies thought that this sounded more attractive than Dandy Hill, which is where these hotels actually are. The card was sent from Nottage Cottage on 26 September 1912.

Nottage seems to have been a popular name as there was also a Nottage House near the Stanley Hotel (see page 87). Nottage is actually a village in south Wales so why it became a popular name for a house in Port Erin seems obscure. May Bank is much more obvious. The bank behind the photographer is very steep and once had a number of hawthorn or may trees on it. Because hawthorn wood is very hard it was traditionally used in boatbuilding for items such as tool handles and rudders which had to be strong for their size. Hawthorn blooms in May, hence its alternative name, but, although very pretty, it was considered unlucky to bring hawthorn blossom inside a house. Those who did so could expect illness or death to follow.

Myrtle Hotel. Again a middle panel from an HEH Ltd. commercial postcard (see top caption on page 87). Myrtle grows naturally in warm areas such as South America and Australia, but Bog Myrtle, a cousin in the same genus, is found in swampy places on the Isle of Man, such as the Ballaugh Curraghs. Its Manx name is *roddagagh* and it was often used as a traditional insect repellent. At first glance Bog Myrtle can be mistaken for a small rhododendron or laurel bush. It has the most amazing but very strong smell.

GREETINGS FROM
"MYRTLE"
DANDY HILL. SOUTH PROMENADE
PORT ERIN *Isle of Man*
H. E. Howorth, Ltd. Fleetwood.

The guest house has now been divided into two dwellings. Bay windows seem to be ubiquitous in Victorian buildings but until the end of the nineteenth century building regulations stated that ground floor windows had to be flush with the exterior wall. In 1894 the Building Act allowed windows to project from the façade and Victorian builders used them to make rooms look larger and better lit.

103

Erin House, like most of the rest of the buildings on Athol Park, was built around 1900, although the road was not adopted until much later. The photograph left, was probably taken in the 1930s possibly to advertise that Erin House was now offering private apartments and was not merely a guest house! Note that the proprietors are standing on the top step. The photograph was taken by the Keig photographic studio, a famous Manx firm run by the same family from the 1860s until 2010.

The second old photograph is the middle panel from a commercial postcard (see top caption on page 87) and proudly sports a phone number. The first telephone service opened on the Isle of Man in 1889 and, by 1901 had 600 subscribers. Phone calls between the island and the rest of the UK became possible on 28 June 1929. Phones were expensive however, and it was not until the 1960s that they became relatively common in private houses.

Erin House ceased being a guest house in 1975, when it appears to have been changed into an old people's home. This ceased in 1993 when the building was converted to flats. Throughout its various changes the building, at least externally, seems to have altered remarkably little.

CHAPTER 5

FUN!

Holidaymakers wanted to have fun, and Port Erin was happy to oblige. The beach with its bathing huts and rowing boats for hire was an obvious attraction, as were the walks in the countryside to Fleshwick Bay and the Sound, but there were others. If swimmers were unwilling to trust to the sea, the Traie Meanagh (Middle Bay) Baths offered open-air bathing in Spaldrick Bay. Advertised as the largest sea water baths in the British Isles, Traie Meanagh was unusual in that it had always allowed mixed bathing – a daring novelty at the beginning of the twentieth century. Galas were held every Wednesday with speed swimming events, bathing beauty extravaganzas, high diving competitions, and novelty races such as egg and spoon and umbrella swimming. And guests in hotels and boarding houses formed teams which, each week, competed for the Squadron Cup.

Land-based sports were also available and Port Erin had two golf links and extensive tennis courts. Again these were both sports which allowed women to take part. In fact there had been an explosion of interest in golf and tennis for women during the last quarter of the nineteenth century. Many a holiday romance, or possibly something more permanent, was able to flourish on the golf links or tennis court.

In the evening there was a choice of venues for entertainment. Collinson's Café had a famous ballroom, as did the Golf Links Hotel: both held tea dances, as well as formal evening balls. The Port Erin Royal on the Promenade was noted for its entertainment throughout the south of the island, as was the Pavilion in the centre of the town. The Pavilion was also famous for its live shows, particularly the concert parties given by its pierrot troupe.

Some visitors to Port Erin came on day trips either by charabanc or bus. Manxland Bus Services Ltd., a subsidiary of Cumberland Motor Services of Whitehaven, opened just behind the Port Erin railway station in 1927 and were the first bus company to cover a network of routes. So successful was Manxland that, in 1929, the Isle of Man Railway Company purchased it to put an end to unwanted competition. Several coach operators were also based in Port Erin over the years, including Challenor, Cregeen, Harrison, Darnill, Dawson, Moore and Duggan, all now no longer operational. For a short period of time (June 1919 to October 1920) Mr Clague even ran a coach company from the Hydro. Another hotel heavily involved in coach operation was The Bay Hotel. R. and N.A. Liddle based their coach operation there from 1919 to 1928, before moving it to Station Road for a further nine years: it closed in 1937.

Harrison's Motors outing outside The Stanley (see page 87). T.E. Harrison was based in Port Erin, first at Ballafesson (1923-8) and then in Station Road (1928-44). For the enthusiasts among us the vehicle shown is a Dodge PLB Duple coach with the registration MAN 24. It seated twenty when it was new in 1935, although seating was increased to twenty two in 1939. As this photograph was taken in 1935 it is possible it was a record of the coach's first outing.

Presumably Mr Harrison was behind the camera.

At one time the terrace of buildings which included The Stanley was called Bay View Crescent after the hotel on the corner (see page 86). According the Porter's Directory of 1889 the crescent also included Busby House, Optic House and Nottage House all of which were private boarding houses. T.W. Barker, the Port Erin stationmaster lived in Busby House.

Breagle Glen Tennis Courts. In 1884 Wimbledon opened its doors to women competitors for the first time in mixed doubles events. Tennis was one of the few sports where men and women could compete together without causing a social scandal. Consequently the tennis courts at Breagle Glen were very popular with visitors and locals alike. The very visible long poles support the protective netting which prevents (most) balls flying into neighbouring gardens.

The tennis courts have hosted a crown green bowling club since 1983. Also on site is a putting green and a rather overgrown crazy golf course.

Rowany Golf Links. In 1895, James Clague, brother of Thomas (see page 53), opened a nine-hole golf course on his farm to cater for the growing tourist trade; few locals could afford either the fees or the leisure to play. Laid out by George Lowe, a professional from St Andrews, it was opened in 1897. It proved popular and William Fernie, another professional this time from Troon, soon extended it to eighteen holes onto Ballakneale estate land owned by Donald Clucas. The postcard is franked in 1913 – the day and month are obscure – and the sender was staying at 'The Level, Colby'.

Just to the left of the photographer is a small tholtan which used to be part of Upper Rowany Farm and is now next to the seventeenth green. It was once known as Crammanagh Cottage (*thie crammanagh*) as it is on a small rise. *Crammanagh* is 'lump' in Manx. The seventeenth hole is known as *Thie Beg*, meaning 'little house', in its honour.

The clubhouse is off to the left and was built in 1912. During the Second World War it became the Port Erin Kindergarten for the small children of internees. Captain and President of Rowany Golf Club was Henry Percy Kelly, High Bailiff of the island, but better known as a fervent ambassador of the Manx language. He became a Welsh Bard in 1920 and a Cornish Bard in 1932.

Today this is the sixteenth hole, Gorse Craig, of the Rowany Golf Course. In 2014 the club considered closure as it had been running at a loss for several years. A reorganisation and cost-cutting exercise meant that in 2017 the club was able to sign a seven-year lease with the Port Erin Commissioners who own the land.

Not far from the golf club is the Traie Meanagh (Middle Bay) Baths. Opened in June 1899, they were built by Alfred Nelson Laughton and operated by him for over twenty five years. Note that on the other side of the bay, building has not yet begun on the Raglan Pier, meaning that this picture must pre-date 1913 (see page 21).

The Traie Meanagh Baths were advertised as being in a sunny wind-sheltered cove and the largest sea water baths in the British Isles. A Tangye steam engine (a standing engine manufactured by Cornishman Richard Tangye for pumping water) supplied 520 gallons of sea water per minute to ensure that the water in the baths was changed daily. Competitions and galas were held weekly, including the Squadron Cup which was for teams from individual hotels.

The baths were purchased by the Port Erin Commissioners in 1926, who ran them for a further fifty-five years. Early in their ownership the commissioners made one contentious change. In 1928 they decided not to open the baths on Sundays, but rescinded the decision three years later. Benches on terraces on the hill provided seats for hundreds of spectators, and were often packed.

The baths closed in 1981, and were sold by the Port Erin Commissioners to Clearwater International Aquaculture for subsequent use as a fish farm. That too closed in 1990.

Unfortunately the stamp, and therefore the frank with its date, is missing from the postcard, but, judging by the wearing apparel, the photograph was taken at the very end of the nineteenth century. The sender, Frieda, says… 'Had this taken after a morning dip. Had a nice swim with Frank the other day. Had a rare time here…' The experience was indeed rare, if not in the way she means, as the pool was mixed bathing – uncommon for the time. It's interesting that the writer of so long ago is actually in the photograph. It seems most likely that Frieda is one of the two ladies in the centre holding cups of tea as they seem the most posed and also the most interested in the doings of the photographer. White letters above the man in the doorway say 'Refreshment room', which allows us to orientate the view. The 'dressing room for ladies' was next door at the end of the building nearest to the photographer.

Sadly the pool has now degenerated into an eye-sore. It is considered to be unsafe and a possible health hazard so is fenced off and not open to the public.

The refreshment room and ladies' dressing room of the previous old photograph is in the background facing the photographer. The board at an angle on the left is a water chute for fun seekers to slide down it to splosh into the pool. The pool had two diving boards, this one at ten feet and another on the other side of the pool at thirty feet. The board and chute in the photograph can be seen in the bottom right-hand corner of the photograph on page 110. The style of swimming costume – the gentleman in the  middle looks particularly natty – dates this to around 1900.

No-one seems to know what to do with the site now, although Hugh Logan Architects (HLA) have proposed redeveloping it into a 'marine recreational facility' including a small hotel, café, dive shop and harbour for small boats. In 2016 planning permission was also granted for a five-bedroom dwelling to be built on the site.

Collinson's Café started life as Spaldrick Bungalow and was designed by Clement Williams and Sons. T Collinson and Sons owned several places of entertainment in Douglas and intended this to be another. It was completed in June 1913. A semi-circular ballroom famous for its sprung floor was added in the 1920s, and the café had its own small orchestra.

Collinson's Café, Port Erin, I. O. M.

During the Second World War, Port Erin with Port St Mary became a giant internment camp, Rushen Camp, for female aliens and their children. For a short time Collinson's became the camp's school until it could find premises where classes could be held in separate rooms. The building continued as an academy for adult internees who could learn subjects as diverse as handicrafts, elocution, gymnastics and languages.

Collinson's café was a branch of a chain of north of England tea shops founded by Thomas Collinson in Halifax in the 1830s. The Collinson's chain had begun as a retailer of tea and coffee but later sold biscuits, confectionery and cakes too. Most of the shops had cafés attached. Collinson retired in 1876, but his sons Joseph and Edward carried on the business, Joseph as what today would be called the 'rep' and Edward looking after the warehouse and administration. Compare this photograph with the one on page 67. The road crossing the field in the centre looks very new and might have been recently laid.

Collinson's café eventually closed, probably in the 1960s. The building was used as offices for a while, and then converted to a dwelling in 1970. It is currently owned by multi-millionaire Jim Mellon, executive chairman of Manx Financial Group PLC, which includes Conister Bank and Edgewater Associates.

The Hut Cafe and Grounds, Port Erin, I.O.M.

Bradda Glen Café, known as The Hut was purchased by Collinsons (IOM) Ltd in June 1925 who ran it in conjunction with their café on the other side of the headland (see pages 114-5). By 1926, five tennis courts had been constructed at The Hut and the owners had applied for a licence for both premises in order to be able to sell light wines sherry, cider and madeira.

Inspired by the success of the Howstrake and Cunningham holiday camps in Douglas, in 1929 Collinsons decided to centre a holiday camp around The Hut (see page 100), although it was still open to the general public for snacks. The Hut also ran popular tea dances and evening entertainments.

Towards the end of the Second World War, when The Hut was still part of the massive internment camp, Port Erin Commissioners held a referendum to find out whether local people wanted Bradda Glen and its Hut to belong to the town. The response was two to one in favour and the glen was subsequently purchased for £20,000. Note: the modern photograph was taken in April 2019, before the Bradda Glen Café was open for the season.

The Hut and Grounds, Port Erin, I.O.M.

In the centre of the photograph, and amidst the crowds lounging at their ease, scurries a waitress. Seasonal tourism requires seasonal staff and waitressing was one of the more popular options for women. Depending on the tips it could also be fairly well paid, which was an advantage as the Manx season was and is short when compared to countries with warmer climates.

Like many Manx cafés after the downturn in tourism, The Hut struggled to find custom during the later twentieth century. In the early part of the twenty-first century it was renovated by the Department for Agriculture, Fisheries and Food (DAFF, now DEFA, the Department for Environment, Food and Agriculture), which is responsible for Bradda Glen. At the time of writing The Hut was being run by the same team as manage the café at the Sound.

Compare this with the view on page 72. More building is visible on the far side of the bay, and tennis courts have been laid out below the expanded holiday camp building in time for the 1926 season. The huts in the foreground may be ones salvaged from Knockaloe Internment Camp – the camp certainly had some – and, by the 1960s, were being used as scout huts. The smoke drifting from right to left in the distance is probably from a steam train en route to or from Port St Mary. The postcard is franked 21 May 1964, and the sender has marked by an arrow where she is staying; it looks to be in the region of Maine Avenue.

Taking the new photograph from exactly the same point as the original would have meant looking directly into a gorse bush so the photographer has compromised. Many of the trees in Bradda Glen, planted as specimen trees, are now of considerable size. This, coupled with a downturn in grazing on Bradda Head, plus fewer people gleaning wood for fires, means that tree cover is increasing significantly.

PORT ERIN I.O.M. FROM THE GOLF COURSE   19048

Ballafesson Chapel, presumably at harvest festival. The first chapel on the site was built in 1794 after one of John Wesley's visits. This chapel replaced it in 1846. The chapel is lit by the hanging oil lamps as electricity wasn't installed in Rushen until 1935. The chapel was refurbished during 1949, when pine pews were installed, instead of the box pews seen here, plus a pulpit which came from Bridge Road, Ballasalla. The celebration service held on 12 January 1950 raised over £500 which largely paid for the renovation.

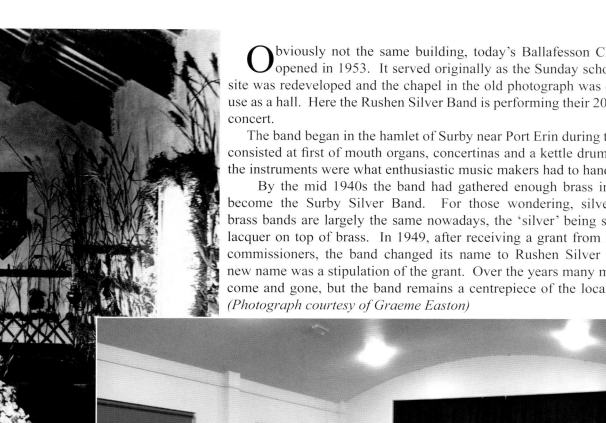

Obviously not the same building, today's Ballafesson Chapel, below, opened in 1953. It served originally as the Sunday school before the site was redeveloped and the chapel in the old photograph was converted for use as a hall. Here the Rushen Silver Band is performing their 2018 Christmas concert.

The band began in the hamlet of Surby near Port Erin during the 1930s and consisted at first of mouth organs, concertinas and a kettle drum, probably as the instruments were what enthusiastic music makers had to hand.

By the mid 1940s the band had gathered enough brass instruments to become the Surby Silver Band. For those wondering, silver bands and brass bands are largely the same nowadays, the 'silver' being silver plate or lacquer on top of brass. In 1949, after receiving a grant from Port St Mary commissioners, the band changed its name to Rushen Silver Band, as the new name was a stipulation of the grant. Over the years many members have come and gone, but the band remains a centrepiece of the local community. *(Photograph courtesy of Graeme Easton)*

Shortly after lunch on 4 August 1939, smoke was seen coming from the roof of Leslie's Pavilion, before flames rapidly engulfed the building. It was known as Leslie's Pavilion after the founder Harry Leslie, a show business manager. The signboard of Darnill's Garage can just be seen through the smoke and flames, and there were fears that the garage too would catch fire.

Not many people now remember where the Pavilion was today. The modern photograph looks south east behind the Erin Arts Centre.

The Rushen Joint Fire Protection Board, as it was at the time, had taken delivery of a new Merryweather fire tender plus a Beresford-Stork light trailer pumping unit, only the day before, but the fire had taken too great a hold in the old wooden building for them to do more than contain it. Note the firemen wearing Merryweather helmets.

Today the Isle of Man Fire and Rescue Service has seven stations, plus an eighth run independently at Ronaldsway airport. Port Erin Station, which serves Rushen, is station 6, based, since March 2019 at what was the Southern Ambulance station in Castletown Road. The Port Erin firefighters, like most on the Isle of Man, are retained, which means that they work part time, responding to emergency calls when needed.

The Pavilion had been adapted from one of the Knockaloe internment camp huts and offered live entertainment which was popular with both visitors and locals. Bands and entertainers visited and there were tea dances and evening dances which many attended in evening dress. In the winter it was used as a picturehouse showing films three times a week.

Taken after the fire, the photograph below records an official visit. The man in the hat, on the right of the photograph, is the island's Lieutenant Governor, William Spencer Leveson-Gower (pronounced 'Loosen-Gore'). Leveson-Gower had become the 4th Earl Granville after the death of his brother on 21 July 1939, only a fortnight before the Pavilion fire. Granville's wife was the elder sister of Queen Elizabeth (later the Queen Mother). Granville was a seasoned sailor having seen active service during the First World War and thereafter, and had acted as *aide-de-comp* to George V. As well as Lieutenant Governor he was also a Vice Admiral, although on the retired list. With the volatile situation in Europe, and the relations with Germany strained, it's possible that Grenville was appointed Lieutenant Governor of the Isle of Man precisely because of his military experience. The island has always been a strategic stronghold in the Irish Sea.

It's remarkable that the building promi-nent on the right in the old photograph above still sur-vives and can still be seen in the middle distance in the new photograph, left. The building in the fore-ground is part of the Shop-rite Living store which closed suddenly in 2017.

Although franked 8 August 1905, the view is obviously one of May Day judging by the May Pole topped by the Royal Standard of the United Kingdom. The marching men in the background appear to be wearing the uniform the British Army wore in the Boer War (1899-1902). On the back of the card the sender has written 'you will find several people you know on this'.

Obviously not a match for location (see page 66 for something close), more a match for occasion. An older Port Erin tradition on the first of May was to visit the Holy Well of St Catherine. An old chapel once stood south of the spring and up to the end of the nineteenth century the spring provided the inhabitants of Port Erin with their drinking water. It can still be seen hurrying down the beach to the sea. Like most holy wells it's credited with healing properties and it's said that the purity of the water was what tempted people to come and live in Port Erin in the first place.

SELECTED BIBLIOGRAPHY

Brown's Popular Guide to the Isle of Man, Anon, James Brown & Son, 1889

A Chronicle of the 20th Century, Vol I: 1901-1950, Various, The Manx Experience, 1999

Cruising Guide to the Isle of Man, Dr Robert Kemp, The James Laver Printing Co., Ltd., 1979

Dive Isle of Man, Maura Mitchell & Ben Hextall, Underwater World Publications, 1994

Friend or Foe?, Doreen Moule and others, Rushen Heritage Trust, 2018

Geology of the Isle of Man and its offshore area, R.A. Chadwick and others, British Geological Survey, 2001

Holiday Isle; the golden era of the Manx Boarding House from the 1870s to the 1970s, John Beckerson, Manx Heritage Foundation, 2007

Island of Barbed Wire, Connery Chappell, Robert Hale Ltd., 2005

The Lifeboat Service in England: the North West and Isle of Man, station by station, Nicholas Leach, Amberley, 2017

Mann Ablaze, Stan Basnett, Leading Edge, 1991

Our Heritage; Memories of the Past in Rushen, Books One, Two, Three and Four, Kate Rodgers (ed), self, c. 1986

Underwater to get out of the rain, Trevor Norton, Da Capo Press, 2004

ACKNOWLEDGEMENTS

The authors are indebted to several organisations and individuals who gave up their time to provide help, information and/or photographic material. They include, individuals: Diane Brown, Graeme Easton, Jim Gibson, Betty Shimmin, James Woolnouth and Jon Wornham; and organisations: Ellan Vannin Images, Harmony Homes, Royal National Lifeboat Institution and Rushen Silver Band.

Thank you all for your help and assistance; any mistakes are entirely ours.